fluttertongue: book 2
THE BOOK
of EMMETT

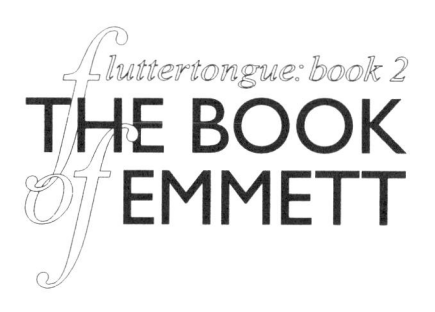

Steven Ross Smith

HAGIOS PRESS

Copyright © 1999 Steven Ross Smith

All rights reserved. No part of this publication may be reproduced, stored in a retrieval system, or transmitted, in any form or by any means, without the prior written permission of the publisher, except in the case of a reviewer, who may quote brief passages in a review to print in a magazine or newspaper, or broadcast on radio or television.

The publishers gratefully acknowledge the support of the Saskatchewan Arts Board in the publication of this book.

Edited by John Livingstone Clark
Cover, design, and layout by Donald Ward

Printed and bound in Canada

Canadian Cataloguing in Publication Data

Smith, Steven, 1945-

Fluttertongue. Book 2: The Book of Emmett

Poems.
ISBN 0-9682256-3-2

I. Title. II. Title: The book of Emmett.

PS8587.M59F582 1999   C811'.54   C99-920185-9
PR9199.3.S5616F582   1999

The Hagios Press
314 – 1121 College Drive
Saskatoon SK   S7N 0W3

for Jill, mother of Emmett

utterings

Furrowed soil draws down into its folds the blond stalks
that spiked all summer toward the sun

Generous river shelters the longnecked, trumpeting flotilla
now wing-tucked, downed to rest, from the long flight south

Labour chamber, storm-charged, attends, to receive
a new being, scrunch-squirming, tunnelling down, down
from the amniotic sea to this shore of hard edges, warm arms
waiting

The Book of Emmett / 9

I heave from the dark
into morning, called to its light
by turbulent squirms
by mewling and sucking

I turn to his kicks, to discovering eyes
I pillow in the palm of my hand, his small forearm
run my fingers in furrows on
his wrinkled brow

he did not wiggle in this nook two weeks ago
the void unnoticed

from emptiness
from fluids
        a life
              is distilled

my fingertip on his miraculous
cheek, the pink curve
of mystery

soothing baby in these late hours
his cries fierce
and unstoppable against my strategies
change a diaper change his clothes change his position
against my body from cradled in the crook of my arm to flat
against my chest lie him on the floor beside me   pick him up
bounce   walk   sway   hum   talk   until I give up
and with him on my shoulder I switch on the computer and
stare at the screen and begin to try to record this in some kind
of poem and he falls asleep interrupting now by offering me a
chance to sleep in 3:00 a.m. quiet
so I lie down with him snuggled to me   his slight unmoving
weight pressed to my chest
stirring a sense of something that is right that I have no word for

as I drift I scan the reservoir of words for the one
and it passes through me   shaped
but naked of alphabet
and its shadow brushes against something I do not know
and as I peer in the dark   the shape becomes
me and my tiny boy
wrapped
in slumber

the heart radiant with light
    and heat. the generosity of it.
    fullness felt at the sight
    of your nine-week old son
    opening his eyes from sleep.
    or the translucent purity
    of the skin of his cheek. or
    lifting his tiny hand to his eye
    his even tinier finger nails
    ignite your wonder
this is light. it fills despite
    its lack of substance.
    you cannot contain it.
at this perfect moment you see
    we all illumine from within.
    you can barely stand the power
    of its brightness, the heat.
you fall to your knees
    press your cheek to his
    press your forehead to the earth
    this light bares you
    exposes you to that
    pain beyond pain that is
    wonder. humility is not the word. you are alight
    with greatness. you are alight
    with all your failings. your incapacities. you
    are alight
    and helpless.

in the dark night   in the delirium
hours after two we rock and walk
and hum around the dining room
no light but the moon   and the stars cascading
in the window and we stop to gaze
out and I lift you from the crook of my arm
up in front of my eyes and your face
becomes another face an alert face a knowing
face   it is a face of clarity   yet I know
that I can never know the mystery.
we are bound in this moment
like no other and we both know   we know and do not
know   but have gazed deep into darkness
and far beyond it   far   beyond

The Book of Emmett / 13

a baby's squeal interrupts the poem.
the pencil becomes less important.
you are living in a fog. of new hours
filled with wakefulness. of many kinds
of postponement and delay. gifts are abundant.
all of them unexpected. an ear delicate as rice paper.
a leg, whole calf and shin you can hold in your palm.
a hand that wraps around the end of your finger.
the wide-eyed concentration, discovery
of the world of objects. the glee.
a bud of tongue through fine lips opens to
a round wide cry, a tunnel
to discomfort you can't identify,
so you comfort.
a feather of breath buffs your neck as you cradle him to sleep.
the pencil has been put down
for this and picked up and put
down   again and again.

in the dimmed bedroom light
you have stripped your baby boy changed
his soiled diaper and now you are cleaning the tiny cave
of his umbilical button   as the cotton tip
probes the still moist healing scab you realize
that this is a gradual closing   sealing him further
and further from the near but distant universe he once
inhabited, the nine-month galaxy this vanished place.
he is here now in this hard world where everything
jars and jabs   and sickness comes in a phone call
from those who fought to protect the river   that stream
of life and the cord comes before your eyes the umbilicus
cut with your own hand that severed your son
from his mother   and now he is here squirming in your memory
on the warming bed in the birthing room   squirming
and fussing beside you in the dark hours
at some discomfort or discontent and his lips
and brow are perfect   you know
you are in the presence of a miracle
and you know his cries will punctuate your lives
for this is the world of pain
where sorrow and lamentation come at you
on every receiver where cruelty is every day
and the saintly ones are snatched away too soon
and you try to understand why you're still here to
scratch at some vanishing thoughts to have this
perfect son who nurses, then wails and twitches beside you
keeping you awake.   you
reach through the darkness for his tiny hand.

The Book of Emmett / 15

information comes ringing
in a call about my loan   and stolen car
the havoc-truth of deficit

is loss where the poem begins?

the car is twisted metal and torn upholstery
confettied with window glass, wrecked,
a toy abandoned by joy-riders

my son is a bundle in my arms and
his mouth   yawning   stretches into a smile that is all light
that floods then flickers, winces to a dark split, spilling sudden
cries 'til his body is fury-shocked, shaking
i rock, rock, will rock him   into calm

autumn is here   the day greying
and cooling   the winding down   familiar quieting   things
disappear, such is expected
unexpected, such
strange shattering

the poem in bits, disguised,
hidden
in this slippage

you are flat tonight, levelled
by doubt, self
shrinking from its passions, you are not
understood, you do not
understand yourself

in her search for imperfection, your lover
has brought you unhappiness
your dog lies on the rug
like another rug
he is a flatcoat
you sigh and shrug
outside the wind chills
you pull the collar to protect your bare neck

a few lingering geese honk, glide and skitter
to the river, not worried
by the coming ice.
just north of here ice is sealing. river
becomes a snake flattening into the silt beneath the steely blanket

you are prone, flat on the couch
your son sleeps in the crook of your arm
this is all you are, all you need to be
a crook'd-arm-hollow with
a tiny heart fluttering against your ribs

The Book of Emmett

A white dusting whispers in the grass.
Winter is discouraging.
If the miracle occurs in whiteness will we notice?
I change a diaper, pick up a tiny sock from the floor.
It seems too common.
Winter forgets the sun is warm.
When I hold him and release my dread, heat returns.
And winter is divine
The miracle is in my arms.
And with soft breath on my skin
love is whispering to me.

Let me tell you how my boy flies. Cradling him in my arms. My foot missing a step on the stair. My hands flying out toward the wall and banister. My boy's tiny body hovering in space, beginning to arc far down toward the hardwood floor. In an instant as long as a photograph I reach for his arm which is flung out in startle and I catch his forearm and he swings like a toy 'til my other hand cups his bum and my arms pull him to my chest as I drop to the stair, terror-shocked. *Dear! Dear!* I cry and his mother rushes to us. *What happened?* I am shaking. We set him on his hand-knit blanket, check him all over. He smiles. Wants food. As his mother suckles him I sob and sob.

The Book of Emmett

imagine that they came and took your son away

you clutch your boy
his face against your neck

there are places where this happens every day

this day
would cinder you
leave enough of you
to burn
next day
and next and next

these places are far from here

you cling
seared
repentant

sucked down
you choke
on the ash
rind

small small boy
you are asleep on the blue futon
your face is turned to me
you are a bright flicker
in this sea of cockeyed
pillows, askew blankets and
the burgundy afghan knit by your grandmother.
you drift in sleep
each arm cocked, each hand up beside your head

you squirm, kick, turn
to me.
you begin to stretch and snuffle and rumble
reaching from the covers toward this day, your seventy-eighth
on this earth   this is your coldest day at thirty below zero
you are oblivious under the comforter
I look and look at you
I say *hello* and smile
I try to understand how love and its fluids combine
then come to this, a life,
then greater love.
hope rests here, on your forehead, as I kiss
you   yes this is purity.
out of love comes life and more
love   but just as sperm in the vagina is at risk and
the blastocyst bouncing in the uterus is
at risk, this moment is threatened
by knowledge of the dark throat

The Book of Emmett   /   21

the sneer, the knife, the jump-bombs,
the devastating shrapnel —
these are images we receive in the news
but you are no image
you live
in my arms
we huddle on the futon together, we
have gained knowledge of love. with it
comes evil.
we are both awake   safe
against the afghan
for now

ice fog rises from the black river
lifts into shapes of slope-shouldered sentinels
humble giants with bowed heads

my shoulders are tight, tense
it is after midnight, thirty below
the car seat is a rock hard bench
my four month old son and I drive the bending road beside
the river a ride to calm both of us
to distract him from his frenzy
and to rest my exhausted patience

the river is black as the chasm we crashed into at his bedtime
the river is quiet
it is a dark vein in night's coal black cleft
but for the curve we follow it is a place I am separated from
by season and by night
yet I hug its flank and dream of summer tranquillity
it is a bending and pulling place where my paddle dips
and I glide quietly in the green canoe
the river is a dream tonight
and I the dreamer drifting in this dark
my son, asleep seconds after the car's first lurch forward,
drifts in a baby dream.
oh to know his dream, a dream
where I am not impatiently putting him to bed
we are at peace together riding on the river
together. my son, me, and the river

The Book of Emmett / 23

but we dwell in separate realms. he. I. the river.
and the sentinels, rising
reminding me that we are watched over
reminding me of time, the huge dark absence of time
reminding me of my senseless impatience
bending me
with my black shame

our son cries in fury and frustration
we cannot understand, find a solution
I pick him up, wrap him close to my chest inside my big sweater
his compact body in my arms
his pale face cowled, peering ahead
tears streaking his cheeks

he sobs, sighs
I have found the antidote, enclosure, burning warmth, my
chest against his back
his small bald head beneath my chin
the sweet balm
our wrap-ture

his head tips against the rib of the sweater
my hand cups his forehead and cheek, he sighs again
against my palm, dozes

nothing that began this is clear

now, this clarity

the goldeneye stays. defies winter, swimming
in the river at twenty below

perhaps the authentic way is here.

today snow beads and rolls off my boots, snow
whispers to me.
i can barely hear, gone deaf times before this
on sirens, on thundering rocknroll.

how to listen in this deafness.

what is the message of the biting wind.

how to know what my son says in his cries
how to hear the cries of all suffering in this.

i walk beside the river. the shifting
ice and water. sun-glint on both.
i give in to the freeze. the melt.
i watch the bold black and white goldeneye, attend,
strain to hear the music of water and ice, the song
of the swimming bird. i give
myself to this.

the music and whispers come clear:
go to your son. become humble. don't pretend.
forget pressing tasks. attend him. hear his squeals.
contemplate the blue veins of his delicate eyelids.
the fragile circles of his tiny wrists.
the perfect, the immaculate
soles of his feet

open

wide

not like anything
but itself
with new vigour

lift

you are lifted as you walk

everything is melting

or lifting:
ice-armour,
snow to its ashcoat,
spirit,
in this false spring.

your coatings cease to resemble
bondage
or dirigibles.
states change
solid to liquid
river open   water
yay! buoyed spirit
springing skyward

a shackle snaps
(you were ready to)
the metal universe
clamp-trap-teeth-winter
gives   you walk shoulder-light
spright-footed

at your back
at distance
your son, your lover,
your worry
he grows too slowly
nutrients melting from him
ash-shadow under his gleaming eyes
worry shades you
false-light?
false-shadow?

what to believe in
how to till faith

still winter

tilt-world

aperture

hurtle

praise

flutterings

2.

    this done. how social to get and how Hendrix thinks
through you in amplitude. this heat critical. that wow.
wondering your head. your head. always this or aching. sing.
soar. chant everything. right there. spirit in a baby's
wriggling. hot these days. these post-modernities rewriting
everything against itself and the spatter and gaffe hooking in
the new redundancies. say it new. now. how? field full of
questions. rock. hard. reminders of matter. what does? slap
and crawl. palm on floor. hardwood. scuttling knees redden.
and purpling skin. age haze. purple greatness. too young to
know brazen songs. the un-sense of form. firming up as I rail.

4.

    jazzy salvage. go to the razed place. the unpremeditated midden. midway there make a turn for the verse. then back. to the dark museum of unforeseen speaking. houses wrecked or for sale to distract. cash and borrow. crash overhead will draw you to it. your baby's cry. wails beyond these margins. go. burrow into another hot one. vegetable syntax. so hot. the difference between tomato and potato growing. light and dark. what task for poetry. such overburden antidote to the techno-market. marked words in Paz's *Voice* book. *sukra, bliss, beatify*. wait. beware the agent hustle. cradle an instrument. pause. stay lean. hear the cast-off home. blowing octaves through us.

8.

Blaise cat (after Cendrars) returns in early morning. walks that cat walk, cat breathing, across a neighbourhood eight blocks, into the waking poem. her own transsiberian. full of de Nerval longing. but more determined. how achieved? with mapping, or steps ex tempore? she has awakened feral memory. but the toddling Emmett boy has allergies. blocked baby breath. impulse and particle unseen. but direct. infecting. incomprehensible. Cendrars rode his own train to invent surrealism. nourished himself with flames. flames so distant this problematic morn. something not linking. green envelope. brown paper. mismatch. dander to sensitive lungs. cleared now. though smoke is everywhere. North Ireland. Chechnya. Montana. where is the aura in this soot? not keyed in today. key left in the gypsophelia. baby cries. footsteps on stairs. in the brain stem, feral, reptilian, a blazing restlessness agitates the limbs.

9.

stairs. forgetting the stairs comes to haunt. no not the stairs. the difference, the open door at the top. go Freudian symbolic. *discovery leading to unconscious.* all mind. never mind. what's thudding in the chest is not a symbol. you were preoccupied with perforations, manuscript and tearing. my god! he's whimpering at the top. you leap. address yourself as *idiot.* clutch. beside the saint of air's tumble. shoulder shut. thud. thanks to all deities invoked. everything moving forward stopped to lean on the doorframe and cry. stare. your head swims. knockout stars in your eyes. the saints sitting on your shoulder at sight's periphery. a word was framed in your thoughts last night, one letter making all the difference. (your friends were carving fish.) difference like a tiny hinge. almost invisible. swings. which way? you forget everything you've read or known. forgetting in the whimper of hinge movements. time hung. fate swung toward you without any words. without any letter that could make a difference. just a tiny body. held. all the difference.

10.

sweat even here. the baby's back turned to me. his mother's back turned away. a disagreement the train clicks through. hauling away any logic. doctor talking about sterile fluids, infected fluids, drainage, baby's passages too small. infected I am by some seeming manipulation. wet in the crease of my neck. sultry if a movie. fluids rule us. pop culture seeps more insipid than water. oil. baby twists in his sleep. not movie. fanning oscillations. fed up. depressed. who cares? somebody else's rules I'm forced to play by. play ball. glove it. gee. love it. keep your eye on. who's on? keep on taking pills. swallowing if bitter. learn. how to? the constructive response. instead of sinking. hold your spot. *you manipulate yourself.* rounding third. glory there as the coach winds his arm like train wheels. legs churning for. heart straining for. passage narrows. baby rubs his ear. cries out. harrowing. home.

11.

    charge running low. critical lack. think about family lines.
such this is. a picnic. generations. devilled or chopped egg.
different as this verse. misunderstood under the cottonwoods
by the lake. on the table the block print table cloth. mother's
gift. the crawler's little hand in the dirt in the mouth. he goes
fast now, on all fours. setting tangents. sit down to lunch.
wind across water. all sensation sifts through something else.
slip your finger past teeth to remove the stick. write fast.
words hold you up. this is a stick-up. not for currency offered.
for some other. unrecognizable. this is not a game. stain
makes familiar foreign. that lineage again. the grandma
game. the thrill. sandwich filling. mould spots thawed bread
blue. slot the words critical. break this, still too familiar. push
that family thing again. give the language dis(syntax)intry.
discomfort gets crucial.

12.

    in listening you construct a language. days in attention. to the true meaning. harken. build. your family has done its ciphering. your son is doing this before your eyes. with four consonants. one vowel. only he and sometimes you understand the narratives. break down as they seem to in time. anguish. held back. the cat harnessed closer to home. can't break free. goes listless. chooses sleep over hysteria, in the wisteria bed. the mystery of flowering. son-speak. loops and repeats consonantal drift. direction. rift. raft into the flow. ruffle of fluff. cat, queen of beasts. licking. rough tongue. your tongue aching to break through rumble into sense. onto thunder over plain. speaking. or at least, listing. leaning to it.

13.

    something about Emmett. or another child. escaped (the thought). realized something about this structure today. the music. lost it then. ruckus in the brain. Why can't hold? realize — ambition is greater than this can be. broke/n.
                                          at
every stroke. hammer age. this raucous pop bludgeon. and poetry surrenders. ten months old, the child is magic. back to the poetry garage where the engine is apart. I want new construction to escape generations of benign expectation. illusionist hands over an empty case. cast string. under upper eyelid, a mote. I want release. e. e. cummings would have somewhere clever to go in verses. vases. Vosges. voices. what you see is what you want. that child. speaking to me. in a thought's vanishing. tired. the family gone. brush, brush. lint away. family dust. the glance settles on all dancers in the light. motivation by confusion for the big trick. elephant big. family big. the pachyderm pops. like a needled sack. can't be mirrors. plucked. gone.

14.

Steven and his boy Emmett. pencils. chew the end. it comes to me just after the walk and out of the shower. as sun fingers the hills. such velour. infant Emmett he is, and contemplate another. just a few seconds, a glance at impossible labours. then this pulse, 'im, I'm catching. yes remembering Jill in labour at forty, me fifty. can't think another one. really. hot today. perfect summer. Marlatt's *Ana* open. women's *heads are full of other people's words*. when not, for anyone? Olympic, this struggle to new, renew. muscles are weary, ageing at leaps between poetic forms. blow. in, out, in. or linger in the leathery rustle of cottonwoods. god here. son so far north of my hands, eyes. lover north too, of all of me. rather be north, but history calls. close work. birds keeping distance. flight path an illegible scribble. that pencil again. in air. in hand. in his beautiful mouth. love. never knew love like this. no. helpless. perfect. nan-nan-mum-mum-gahgn-gahgn-gahgn. language from his holy mouth. gives. makes me give.

The Book of Emmett / 39

16.

shoot. shoot. star. streak sky. Perseid Purcell music.
Bernie-cat calls outside my window. such longing. dinner,
drinks, earlier. anorectic drama. all evening. hunger for
identity. strike. yearn. son too far from my arms. eyes. days to
go. sleep twice turn off the machine and drive. alas. mere
miles. Mir far away. moons of Jupiter. last observatory chance
roofed up under the dazzling sky. pulse in that familiar place
(fading) in me. old habit. instinct passing into chase. your
move. the unsureness of a poet's step in the dark. shoeless.
nobody everybody speaks to me. her slim body amber eyes
speak. old habit. choose the beach chair. far from water. from
anyone, anything that matters. everything overhead. overheard
too many words. a woman mad, not mad. hungerthin. fluid on
the ear twists my boy's nights into knots of cries and pain. my
wish for easy answers. not tubes. as stars swish past. I sit still.

17.

    impressive. the highways ministry is building overpasses for animals. red flags. dozers. jackhammers. I'm driving. they'll need maps, the wild ones. my son is an angel, flew above these mountains. rock looks plasticene-forged. Pleistocene and older. pines spike. speech is beyond me. left to company. construct what you will of syntax. Olson knew. maximized poetics. thick in them. driving though packs of them split by my highways. wild and lost. man cold. man hot. hell. countering is impossible with this narcissism no matter how earnest or eco-minded the driver. my son, do elsewise. I have managed only myself. and a few lines. I'd face them if I could see behind the cloth. known lies scar and lynch. I'd rather the lie of unknowing. the trying. something I give you angel-boy. something to angle to in your way. you give light. all of us awe-struck, negotiating heavy equipment. lost. to the wild elegance.

18.

    son restless. sentry trees surround. centuries of bark and reaching. water all around. you worry about fuel depletion. your own. you keep on. the dinner party continually interrupted by his hands or legs. another day like the one before. so rare. walking symposium with Daphne. the gaps, the leaps, that are possible writings. in any direction. not to move through space, but in it. that's it: *authentic*. in-ness. the water so warm in the rocky pools. hands immersed. reaching for shimmering stones. Mount Baker in a mystic haze. Emmett eats sand, becoming a salt addict by the sea. the resulting diarrhoea. you are a worried parent. worried by the beach in his belly. but amazed. you see in his face discovery and joy. see struggle's earnest brow. you call him *sandy bumwad*. he refuses sleep. flopping to the pillow to rise again and smile. you are wearied by all his activity. the shadow across the pale dry meadow makes you look up. an eagle or raven gone over the treetops. you await its cry, for identity. something wells in you. eyeglint. a just-too-late glimpse. beyond naming. gone. time to restep in full attention, refill. turn to restless heart. walk the line the symposium talks. lingual line. stop in the arbutus grove. the talk there all amber, rust, and green splash. white fire in Daphne's hair. you're caught in the flare of her words burning in electric eyes. amber-fused.

19.

    there are poems in the things I cannot name. long roads away from home. lone camping at the lake of the two jacks. father calls along the yellowhead. calls our house, just hours before his arrival. days before mine. all surprise and unpredictability. rough roads. wind shushing the trees into restlessness. in the dark I've been driving through the mountains, my ear aching. trying to listen. the poem punching the drum to be heard. it's not that easy. Emmett and his mother both crying in the phone. the ear takes it all. and the puncture flattens any chance of momentum. earlier I thought about the poem's integration. what fits? will I sleep dry? earlier, jacking up the car, reading instructions. slot, head, wrench. it doesn't sound good. sounds like rain on the tent. in bear country. don't feed them or pause for a photo. how dark among the eco-shoppers. I'm just looking for a meal and a phone to call home to the tears, the desperation. me out here close only to this. among the jacks — pine, lake. lift the phone, the eyes. comes to hoisting in this vertical land. lift this from itself. *Emmett, Jill, don't cry.* nothing ready, not to worry. some people locked to their own intention. blindered. poems with or without intention get written. get it all wrong. no amount of hand-wringing or wrenching will help. all are blameless. one day a call will startle us with a name set free of its body. road closings and detours. handshadows. clockless. the tent walls. a dark flutter.

The Book of Emmett

23.

why is the darkness so earnest, so overriding? what burr burns in the hide? reality hides. eludes the means of language. *no* is everywhere, black noise that drowns all joy. go there. to interrogation. to the ash-trace. breathe in. exhale. your air stirs a fine drift. black and white flakes float to your cheek. in the mirror the smudges speak to you. wordless. your life taken over by loss. though every day of your child's life is a growing miracle. you are absent from your self. perhaps the loss is of a younger you. now your gestures, your stammerings are directed, but not by you. you are accused. you are in crisis. you are in the season of the holy birth. you are dry ash. tearless grief. ash-trace. smudge is pain. to face it, rub the blackness in until it pales, move your mourning tongue through the dust. through the wound let come the deeper pulse, lips poised for speech all the while. begin with air pushed across the lips. invent a syllable. hear the parable alive in your own son's squeal, *up*, his pointing arm. lift your eyes to follow. ceiling, light-star. whisper to him of, after loss, what remains.

26.

I am in love. sundogs flare this morning as I drive my beloved across town. this is a novel kind of love. barely the beginning of a novel of love. he cries with sun in his eyes. I drive past the car with frosted windows dawdling in the passing lane. we are late. this morning was all fuss. dogged resistance. I am too worn down for politics. or much more crying. he stops crying when the angle changes and his eyes are shaded. sun and ghost. suns out of range. science comes before my radio ears. with a glycerine and ink disappearing-reappearing experiment. all things part of *that-which-is*. separateness does not exist. good news for lovers. and my beloved sits over my right shoulder, proof in the car-seat. sixteen and a half months old. father-son romance, untethered. feelings that flood or flare in the unexpecting heart. who writes this novel? description incompatible with what he wants to say. but that twisting resistance burns to the core. *all right.* I throw the pants to the floor. *don't wear them.* promise to myself broken, with anger. the power struggle. love? I want to overpower him. I want to keep driving. where? destination incompatible with where I want to go. the magic of it. the unempirical haunting. his tears, not glycerine, but salt. stopped. I lick one droplet with my tongue. that soft tang. I watch the moist streak dry. a thin, almost invisible crust forms a trace, seen in angled light, on his flushed cheek. sundogs bound from the sky.

The Book of Emmett / 45

28.

    Emmett duck-walking. red and blue snowsuit baby waddle. back and forth on the riverbank above the weir. we are at his pace. that way and this, and back. I am patient. everything gleaming in midday sun. yes, I am patient, but keen for a view of the island. *this way*, I say. Emmett toddles, turns to me, laughs as I wave, *this way*.   I crane to that island mid-river. earlier, cycling the trail, my eye caught a shape there, shadow-grey against pale snow, whiffing a swimming duck.

        Emmett's world is nose-close, at hand's reach. he bends to probe a chunk of shabby snow. he knows little of the hunt, of the distant gaze.   coyote lowered his nose, loped along the shore. the goldeneye duck churned water between her and the wily shuffler. I cycled home, dressed my son, grabbed the sleigh and binoculars, headed to the river.   Emmett wobbles, meandering the trail. I check all directions for baby hazards. train the lens on the island. no movement. *this way*, I call again. Emmett grins, detours. we both giggle at the mischief of coy distance. down the trail a stranger approaches. my eyes shelter my boy. I edge to him. the man, grey-haired, brisk in white shoes, moves between us. *partner*, he says, *that boy makes you the richest man in the world*. Emmett scoots to me. words fall apart in my mouth. I nod. the stranger walks on. coyote and goldeneye sheen beyond sight. son shimmers in my arms.

29. for Robert Kroetsch, Miles Davis, and Richard Stevenson

    I would drop into the wordless world, world of silence
and gesture. but for weakness. I have been praised. makes me
addict to words. *the silences in Miles Davis — the cry*, RS
said. I am too favoured. dreamt through the poem to erotic
encounters. the matron's bare leg over my knee. the articulate
grammar of flesh, a murmur. silence growing loud with
desire. the pressure to time your utterance. to ejaculate with
precision. with no rules but my own instinctive will. I caress.
I stop. draw out of lust into the taut light.   later I'm stretched
thin across the morning by my son's resistance, his twisting
body that fights the intention of my hands, even my offered
heart. the act of dressing becomes war. my hand raising to
swat his bare behind. we are bound before words. feral.
fierce. fretful. I turn away. step *from the prisonhouse of
silence to the world of speech.* speak gently, slowly in to
the fraught space. beware the slap. chatter-trap illusion of
escape. listen. the trill. wail. the cry. the call. that Munsch
scream. that terror. at what is. what is almost done. what
is absent in all the noise. Miles, the measure of spirit in
your breath, lips to the horn, waiting for the phrase,
floating line, that brassy prayer. *the cry of its occasion.*
I hear from the moment's prisonhouse. I am imperfect.
I walk across the room, my hand cuffed to my pocket. away.
I regret my thin veneer, my ready fuse. I am raw. scraped
by the glissing note. the papery brush scuffs my skins. I am
punctured by the ivory blade. this music grates.

Miles, what now? the thin whisper of your horn-voice drifts
against tempo. pulls through the measure. speaks, unsilenced
by silence. RS? RK? what to do? the poem does not help me.
my shoulders are an iron bar. my temper crinkling aluminium.
cool, cool, I tell myself. your notes, Miles, stretch me now.
temper that metal. fathers, all of you, come to me in this
discordant room. we are all sons. open the barred cell. draw
me to the intervals of silence hidden in the thicket of noise.
give my son one perfect note. let us heed. the cry, the desire,
aching with love.

33. for Robert Kroetsch

digging in Derrida for Celan time, the secrets of clockworked hands, stoneworked hands. fingers bent to mark the passing word. memory scripted into the worked earth. my son becomes my memory. as your mother, RK, does not remember you are not yet born in the photograph you clutch on your fifty-sixth birthday, of her at seventeen. echo fixed in mouth and eyes that trace the becoming one. in a photograph today you, near seventy, are almost smiling, with her lips. calendar is circle. my son laughs and I am young again, grinning, in his face. memory forgets time, articulates its loss in particulate light. I reach, my fingers are waxen, melting in the current. from the river a bird I have forgotten in winter's exhaustion calls. its epaulets flash red on bobbing cattails. my boy squeals. I write *red-winged blackbird, E's first*, *South Saskatchewan River*, in the book you gave me, Robert, in Banff in '94. I was forty-nine. *A Bird Lover's Life List and Journal*. first birds remembered there. E was a trace in my eyes I couldn't yet see. a turning page is a fluttering wing. the clockwork wheels spin in many directions. the poem is the place we all want to be led to, moss or sage greening in the soil at our feet. I ache, blame it on time. the dark bird cries as yesterday and tomorrow. I scribble, awkward, holding pen and rock. my son, sitting in the grass, sees it fly, says *bid*, *bid*, and when the bird disappears he waves his small hands back and forth, fingers stretching toward the blue, says *ky, ky*. this is the poem. for a moment today, was it today, I thought it was mine.

35.

    crow call creaks out of dreaming into the delirium of morning. crashes to the ground of domestic dispute. black drama at departure acted for an audience gone draws me to its theatre till I retreat from the melée. the tears and accusations. the crushing of mellow. crow calling through all those fictions. blows through the air out of the brush. that clamour. undercurrent. airlift. the clattering wheels retracting into the wells. I am flying Saskatoon to Winnipeg to Ottawa on the plane with Elijah Harper. the eagle feather held to the nation flies in memory. Elijah, smaller, more frail than he seemed in pictures.　everyone frailing in the friction that wears. turbulence in the air. the tumble. crow's wings in tatters. flying over so many lakes. lake I grew up beside. lake of Gerry's remembering that leads to the Skeena. I have so little to say in this lake of rarefied air. yesterday I bobbed in a concert with hundreds of children screeching with glee, and saw the ones who will keel in the current when I will be gone and forgotten, though my son may recall my face, my faces. all the ones I show him in love or anger or anguish. some traces of gestures that will drift in his mind beyond ash. this dreaming riff of fingers over keys, a vanishing energy fired by a collection of cells that happen to be me. thinking. O Elijah, O Gerry. O black bird. O silver bird. O my son. O lover. O stage of dispute. O unnameable one. this would be strong were I stronger. this would be prayer were I more able.

40.

that summer. summer of clustered starfish static in rock cavities beside Active Pass. that gone summer, slipped to the underside of memory until my son points at the wet sidewalk two thousand landlocked kilometres eastward and says *purple starfish*. I try to explain distance until my knee aches. until I realize that starfish can shine anywhere. I should have known. I have read poetry (and about it) and know something of meaning outside words, of association and leaping. this morning is too stiff. fluid in the joint hampering the torque. though the sun warms and the leaves are a stunning backlit russet gleam, summer is done. poetry is closed up in the books on my shelf. I have avoided it, caught in cavities of necessary duty. in the rush and narrowing only one thing is sure — propelled, I know nothing of propulsion, except for the ache. I want to give up right here.   birds flicker in the tree's skeleton. sparrow and nuthatch. they are a hundred times more energetic than I, despite their hollow bones. starfish glistens (his bones must be soft), hugging the sidewalk at the centre of Emmett's trance-fixed eye. definitely purple.

41.

it is simple, really. the milk carton, empty. he's cranky in the morning. these two not related. forgive me. imageless. empty of . . . pictures? sight? the eye wants to anchor back. against the governing *thrust*. well, not exactly. let's say *hesitant nudge.* this striving for a disintentioned sprawl. pushing past the barrow or bough. amnesiac. disinfoming as I move. I cough. my hands stiffen to the breath. none of this is like poetry. it is easy to delay, the vessel empty. a yellow egg sits on my sill. it is the shape of eternity. there is no centre at this edge. that bush flaming in my eye reminds me I have come up to morning light. wind is brisk. fingers slip. you were angry with delay. furious. used up by the slack. I recompose, listen, but the notes are imperceptible. my ear is plugged. damaged drum. *pardon me* does not help as I am striving to hear beyond. or am I deceiving myself? nothing helps. the pouring milk is soundless. what can you expect of a vacuum? everything fills, corrects itself eventually. doesn't it? blue jay jackhammers the sunflower head. gulps. is gone in a cerulean flash. what is the order of things? I have no coffee. black, it's a void I can't stomach. everyone and all their conversations are drifting to my cochlea. why can't I hear? so much for distant whispering. so much for black and red and dependency. even the jay does not shriek. I put on my coat. cough in chilled air. walk through my breath to the store.

43.

I've been thinking about you. all your words. all that pushing away I've done, you've done. and my mind turns, resists even now. where does all this talking come from? who would not listen? Father, the air full of thought or word can be a vacuum.

my son is tiny. I gaze at the nape of his neck, look down on the top of his head. I am filled with tenderness. thinking *beauty*. beauty that terrifies. love that fills me. cuts me down at the knees. I am weaker now. I want to lie down. Father, did you feel this way?

I am tempted by metaphor. that skilled gloss on pain. or an image. there are few here. I lower my nose to his crown. draw in that sweetness. Father, did you do this with me?

today I am torn to bits with responsibility. but I take you with me into this fray. your walking speed has slowed, you tell me. when you walked around that lake in Florida, what did you remember of my young skin? what will I remember of my son's? great blue herons grace that lake. I know. I walked with you. I gazed at these birds. you looked inside your mind, straight ahead at the path. you talked of the world. the bird took my breath with its elegance. my son was not yet born.

the heron is a wader, often solitary, focused and single-minded. poets dance on the rim of our ears. I look at your wedding picture. there I am an unseen gleam. I think of your nose buried in flesh   my Mother's, my own. this is the giving up. the surrender. the terror. helpless love. how we avoid this daily.

the heron is on the South Saskatchewan river, latitude 52 degrees, stark still on the east bank where not many walkers go.

the heron is at Cain beach on Georgia Straight, latitude 48.8 degrees, skirting the rocky shore.

the heron is on Lake Hollingsworth, latitude 28 degrees, knee-deep near the reeds, as we walk by.

shrines. so easy to talk our way past. the bird probing the shadowy water. we barely see.

stop. look with your son. son, look with me. gaze into the deep ache we bear. bare.

45.

the writing. it is not an adornment. not hobby. is core. is not what you do in the wistful morning. or that late-night word-sweep. it is you. you in the current of meditators. you who reaches beyond entertainment and investment portfolios. you who seek the unquantifiable place. beyond the bleak and selfish. you live out the writer rather than fit him in. you are not a time slot, or keyboard or genius. damn cold today. you could tell by the stinging ears, numb forehead. this line of thinking stops you. no inspiration here. who cares about the weather or your snagged thought lines? certainly not those birds — house sparrow and northern flicker — jockeying at the bird bath. they see a world completely different from your own. they understand Wittgenstein. they will perpetuate in spite of, even without, your strained thinking. everything slipping through the sieve of time. you have not been reading enough poetry. too much aboutness. only as an infant did you live in a state of pure experience. with the mouthing of language began loss. it is all you have. it is nothing. with each word you move farther from experience. hence the wisdom of the silent orders. knowing what you cannot know when filled with words. full of words. full of loss. speaking of a place made up. built on words. that substanceless substance. Sorrentino loves digression, the looping leap even further from innocence. Sorrentino who reaches across the water to be young again. to rediscover orange before he knew its name. pure. when he could laugh. before the words and memory soaked everything into their serious holes. porosity.

The Book of Emmett

you crawl down the tunnel of a sponge. your tongue dry. the
flicker tilts his head back, his bill to the sky. at thirty below
the water feels warm sliding down his throat. are you making
all this up, because you can say it? what of this scene without
its words? what is being made up that you have no words for?
you laugh at yourself. you are no philosopher. you are a dull
mind. your tongue is dusted thick with toxins. Robert Johnson
is still singing from his grave. *dust my broom.* his tune fusses
at your ears with something beyond the words. might be pure.
pure digression. watch for it. *I want to watch* says Emmett
reminding you of Peter Sellers' Chauncy, who *likes to.* and in
another garden Gunnars' rose nods and feathers its scent into
the air. and all this? all these black strokes filling this white
space. this clutter, detritus. who cares? it is all made up. *up*,
Emmett pointing at the light. nothing but light. spectral waves
and minute particles. all make illusion. Wittgenstein again,
everything we see could also be otherwise, and if this is so,
description is a lie. but you know this. lying through your
teeth. biting down on the emptiness. you speak quickly to
deceive the tongue. to fool yourself back before the grit-taste.

46.

I am trying to remember. get my whole life in here.
realizing that most of life is memory. memory and the split
second. poem, not the remembered, but memory itself.
memory fore and aft. poemory. pomme du jour (keeps the
doctor away). fruit of the day (*of the unblinded window*). a
core of clues might be found unexpectedly. a hidden seed
jabbing from a chewed husk. in a greeting on the screen
where Fred said *Gung Hey Fa Choy*. no hint but a spinning
tongue. a whole conversation reels under stacks. conversation
that blew open the doors that still swing in my ear. swing like
Louis and Ella slipping in a mote you don't hear until the
fourteenth listening. blows then through like a headline
spinning my head to the grace note. peripheral. comes centre.
impossible to face, to live up to, what you know. in a lifetime
I plod between perhaps seven upliftings. the rest is *scree-
slipping* (to borrow from Wah). ta-da! I think it's the New
Year he's offering me. even these slip away and you forget
until the next one. in this recall I would have to write about
deep night because, since my son was born twenty-seven and
a half months ago, I have visited every hour of the dark. this
morning he woke twelve times between 6 and 7 a.m. driven
by his little legs to leap from bed, his feet beating across the
hall bearing my own psychic battle on the crest of their
scurry. I'm able to remain relatively polite. but this is about
poetry. in his note Fred mentioned tapes. three mornings of
poetic conversation laid down in cafés. etched into the oxide-
dusted acetate. three days that change my life. remember?
that's what I was talking about. poememory. or at least the

The Book of Emmett / 57

way I write about it. last summer I hiked the trail to the top of Mount Galiano. my chest heaved. thank goodness I know the benefit of vigorous exhalation. I pushed on, spurred by recollection of the serenity that waits at the summit. this is what I lack today. serenity. I fret. I tire of the narcissism of the first person pronoun. I'm getting too verbose. I confess, I'm out of shape. this is a time for resolutions. I will do this and that. I will be spare. I will come to you in different postures. you will recognize me by my stumbling jig and reel. I will be polite. I will seem confused about the hour. dizzy. listing. listening to a distant conversation.

54.

after the illness, fatigue, racking cough. you are a dry,
bare twig. morning bright and cantankerous. teapot lid flying
from his little fingers to smash on the floor. your patience
breaks apart against the baseboard. your voice is loud, angry.
his tears are real but without regret. he is frightened by your
roughness. you bear the regret. such is the dichotomy. patient
love has its breaking. you apologize. love is imperfect. he
apologizes. the lesson like a walnut in your throat. you are not
yet fully recovered from the virus, or imperfection. music
stays distant, perhaps even lost. you fret. though today you
feel like giving yourself a break. you are practising for the
real thing. ideal. perhaps a café break? or make your own and
sit at your desk and try to recover that gist, that groove. you
labour wherever you are. are almost stopped though the light
is so clear. trees breaking into bud. this should be all you
need. a sign of spring. a green and swelling shoot. something
that would flow through this verse. a sucker that would reach
down to new soil and find nutrient mineral. you stand still,
waiting for roots to spring from your feet, buds to break open
at your fingertips.

57. for bpNichol & the fugitive text

an ordinary day. we're on the couch. my son and I. I'm flu worn. you, bp, are speaking in my ear, saying *"ordinary" you draw too much attention to it and it ceases to be; ordinary that is.* Emmett wriggles on my lap, wants to jump on my ribs. we grapple, joyous wrestling, full of grunts and giggles 'til he wears me down and we settle. he leans into the couch back, gazes at me, grinning. I look into his brown eyes, into *that which is.* that which I know but do not know. I want to call it *transcendent, eternal.* it is not *ordinary.* it is not a word. I know that this is the moment I have lived for. everything has led to this. nothing else matters. not even words. language flees. truth is a fugitive that escapes its speaking. the true poem a whisper, wordless, beyond ear's range. in my hand, his hand is soft, alive. and huge in its smallness. I could hold it forever. could hold as we grow toward other moments. never leaving this one. though the day wears down and words insist.

your chanting voice still speaks in me. my tongue hears in its speaking as I search for your words with my lips. I will follow your singing. I sit on the floor, leafing through your texts searching for the one I can hear, intoning pharaohic name shifts across the sculpted rims that separate us now. I am stopped. your text missing, my own voice fled from me. my fingers flicker in the air, itching to press your words to my tongue, tongue flicking them back across my lips. *Generations Generated.* I can hear it but its text escapes me. I would dissolve into that song.

Emmett collapses to my ordinary chest. I gasp, *h-h-u-u-h-h-h-h*, with the force of air driven up from my lungs and across my lips. we laugh. we are one. we are beyond naming. are laughter. singing.

61.

a dog's stomach can turn over in his body. everything
twisted and blocked. blood, gas, and the passage of food. his
world flipped topsy-turvy by fear and anxiety. this morning
your boy was full of cranking and whining. full of himself.
twisting your patience at the name of the day. at toast. at
washing his hair. at choosing his clothes. you raise your
voice, grab his shoulders, hoist him to attention. jar sense into
him. you will extract co-operation. you are the commander of
nothing. you are on a rope and know no way of getting off.
you are too harsh. spur nothing but fright, sadness, regret. you
fret over logic's defeat. you ache all morning. the dog lopes
around displaying his shaved belly and its scar. his stomach
righted inside and tacked to the rib wall. he is more subdued
than before. the scar was bright red at first but is now slight
pink, almost grey, the colour of his skin. your skin is an
astonishing pale organ, stretched thin. over such desperation.

70.

    you tell in fragments. think you make sense. only you know the whole story and what you know is incomplete. your old car is failing. choking up, spitting fumes, stalling, going flat in the rubber. you drive it with perverse pride, though you dream (and do not tell) of shiny new metal moulded over a computerized drive train. you are a secret materialist pining to be in a different story. at the garage they give the tire quick service. you want the mechanic to fire you up with a new poetic spark plug. soon you're back on the road with the old machine not leaking any air. your drive is prodded by the traffic whispering behind. in the mirrors you are aware of John Cage crossing lanes acrostically. of Gertrude Stein divining America. of Fred Wah and Gerry Shikatani skittering the gravel side road. of Paul Celan ghosting in a train in a tunnel underneath. of Daphne Marlatt, stately and fluid, riding in a milkwhite limousine, accompanied by Suka, her chalky Labrador retriever. of Tim Lilburn's pilgrimage, in company with Lao Tzu, John Duns Scotus, and Jan Zwicky (though walking they are always ahead). you wave, take the exit ramp to pick up your son Emmett after his visit to the festival of trees. pine and spruce tarted up with lights and bows. but he loves the glistening baubles and the yellow school bus ride. you cannot write this riding with one hand on the wheel. though you try. cannot guide this story to any sense. it is about green. and about (though not) James Joyce. it is about a Parisian café. the smell of oil and grease. is about love (though this is hard to discern). and a diner in Swift Current. is about Detroit and a wrench and adoration. so far (to the reader's relief), it is not about a bird, or butterfly, or basket (though Gertrude might dispute this). it is, and is not.

75.

yesterday the cut tree limbs began to sprout and bud
despite dismemberment. now my patience is cut from me by a
wiggling boy awake early and into the testing of boundaries.
and the final act of tossing his head, skull crashing into my
cheek. and the shouting. and crying. and apologies. night
barely gone, it is too damned early for any of this. the lump
rises on my cheekbone, so we rise to an icy cloth. later this
morning, the pea-stones are located miles from a beach, the
delivery arranged. now he is all smiles and a runny nose I
keep wiping. endless parental service. control wrested from
me by a miniature me. am I whining? my limbs are wearier
than yesterday. I have fallen behind my own beliefs. the
vigorous wind swirls with grit in this season of uncovered
ground. topsy-turvy. earth, what next, to tilt me when I wish
tedium? *holy cow, heaven's sakes*, he says. I am tempted to
utter *te deum laudamus* in spite of myself.

76.

at morning, the unpredictable musics.

fear creeps, unbidden, over your left shoulder. pain rakes the stressed, thinning bursa of your elbow. engineroar propels terror to your gut. fingernails demand your teethed attention. you fear your cherished one will be taken from you and from himself. you jerk your elbow from the woodhard rest. you are thinning, bufferless. becoming less of yourself as your son grows. you wear away. there is less of you available for fear, but fear is closer, at your neck. one so small becomes more and more of you. (you have given yourself.) becomes himself. you dread, hope never to be borne to, the day of bad news, the unendurable day. day when everything thins, empties, grates. day when the word you avoid, whispers. the cramped day. dare you give it name.
her skin shines with intrinsic sheen. glows beyond speech. she is a longlimbed flirt leaving notes and glimpses of ankle, thigh. you resist. fearful. you are busy. with little morningtime for allure. in no time you fall to the translucence. grey sky brightens, then is blocked by her face at your lips and your hands searching the radiant terrain for its source-light. morning straightens and falls to the bed. this is desire. is convenience. is love. a speechless promise. you roll and buck. she rides. you spin in light, one flame, eyeless, burning where your skins hiss.

you are both dawnings. the glissed note twice gliding. overtones. heartdrum, whispering throat.

78.

    i am speaking. my mind aiming beyond *everyday talk cut off from true being*. my tongue curling on a snowflake. tongue clumsy to symmetry. tongue thick and distant *from true being*. crystal dissolving and lost in saliva. i am unfamiliar to myself. strangeness feels familiar. perhaps it is seasonal, an affliction, a coating. snowfall. snow dusting unsightliness.   with snow i rediscover sledding on a yellow plastic torpedo. my son wants to climb higher and higher on the slope. yesterday was our third time, our highest hill, with frightful speed and bumps and swerves. he is fearless and cherry-cheeked, cheered on by his mum. we are kids keen on slick snow though i take up most of the room on the sled. *blast off* he shouts and we do. we rocket. my heart leaps twice to my throat and i hoot. we careen, keel off the path, are sprayed with snow and tumble into the fluff and he whimpers for kleenex for his eyes but we are mostly laughing and not meditating on *being*, true or false. we kneel for a moment as if frozen to the snow. stand and turn to the hill again. his diminutive shape bright in red and blue, hooded, booted, and gloved, bobs ahead as we huff and slog up the slope. this shape of me. this little man who leads me now backward and forward in time. who slips control and reticence from underneath me. at the steepest part he stops, calls *Daddy* and reaches. i clutch his hand that curls to my palm and we heave up for *just one more*, wriggle onto the sled and *whoop* our truest cry as we bounce and fly over the pure, dazzling white.

The Book of Emmett / 65

82.

"i don't like you," through sleetgrey evening, the glarebarbs scrape. your boy's words, toddle-tongued, aim true. this exchange, coarse coinage hammered through your pores, draws droplets *in the shape of seconds*. bloodclock that lops you. his projectile words, *"i don't like you. you're bugging me,"* causeless. you strain through the wound-sear to smile. you stand, *"hello son,"* corroding on your lips. the pulseclock of your blood ticks time and talks defiant, three years old at your face, facing you with future and past. your blood-son, pure-son, you thought he was imbued with angels. someone said *"intrinsic evil, these little ones,"* to your dismay. yet his little, devilish words, their too big blows bruise, vein-blotch your flesh. his skin, your blood-currency, you see dark falling on it, his heart's unsourceable sadness. *"come here,"* you whisper, *"i have something to tell you,"* opening your veil-arms. *"it will just take three seconds."* he stands still. "*no,*" he says, *"four seconds."*

83. to Paul Celan

i am not different from you, brother. hair combed, eyes gazing ahead. features suitably organized, relatively symmetrical. our skins betray no anguish but each strand on each of us shapes a mesh of horror and grief. how to know this, make it known. let us trace each other's handwalk, cupping, shovelling. we'll dig, bent on stiff knees. yesterday a magnet bent all sound and i was livid. this is all it takes. i lost a toy. not living, particular love (like you). yet your hair is neater than mine. i have seen photographs. i cannot know your pain but see how my son loves his mother. he is besotted and tells me of his rapture and some days wails at being parted from her for a few hours or a few blocks. absence without end. inside each of us a child wails at a fence. it is murder. how we tense. strive to quell. suck ourselves dry of memory. but, brother, you carried with you, every day, without succour, that loss. i am the same, but have been spared chilling incidents, violent severing, the horror-song. no, i could not be the same, as you. i am younger and hardly wounded. i play with my son (as you did) and leaps and laughs fill the air. i thrill. i flex (and am free of cramping). i am only slightly haunted (not hunted). that magnet polarized me, it is true, yet my fury is unconvincing in the force field. it's a question of alignment. humble, presumptuous (and yes, too late), i ask to be your brother, your bothering kin, craving, copying, puttering at your lines and my own. peeking, curious and agape, near your skin, skein of your words, left carved — no — *scraped*, from the flaked air.

85.

ascendance borne of smoke. death-horror. transfiguration through fire and smoke-grit. how the eye stings then lifts. the blot on the day rising, a smoke-trail to saintliness. i have no right to write of this as if it were my own. but the air is not clear here. we are all survivors, grit-borne. grit-boned and aching. yet my son is innocent, fresh, and saintly already. gaining strength, but how soon he coughs. how to preserve his purity in the fray. how to sway him toward justness while he screams on the floor for more brown sugar. a struggle over sweetness feeding bitterness to the tongue. i cannot tolerate cruelty but appoint myself despot. he wails in my domain. on my floor within my hearing. it grates and shatters. i am tempted to enter, to struggle, to pepper the air. i turn on my dictatorial heel, walk away to a space to let be. earlier i said *ascendance*. but we are falling. yes he is my descendant. blood of my blood and flesh of my flesh. yet his own. he will carry it sugared or sullied or serving into a time relieved of me. i wish him to be ash-free, but know that the grit in his mouth will not always be sugar. i speak to myself. *step away, let be. let him have his own gifts.* later i'll place a hand on his spine, with a fingertip i'll dust his lash

88.

poetry is delay. desire is delay. poetry is therefore desire, a continuum of delay. the postponement of D-day. you lie with words, or your lover, and prolong. stretch the line on long and longer, or snail your tongue over her hip circling the ilium crest, the circle itself insisting delay. hey diddle diddle. riddle is delay. the rhyme not speaking of utensils, but of — figure it out — maybe Adam and Eve, and we know what happened to them. or to us lovers. and the little dog never stopped laughing. Emmett laughed and laughed without getting the pun. cresting. Emmett borne before that crest, that pelvic carriage, after the end of delay. Emm plays at the bed-side. *i want to stay up all night*. he delays 'til he remembers the rapture of wishes and whims in stories and rhymes. then wants words and resists the story's end, yet yearns for it. how we love to hover euphoric in curves of words, whispered or gasped. tongue-flit that flirts with our lusty ears. tremble. tremolo. titillation of breath there, in the spiral cavity. in the spell-bound, spinning, spawn of delay. 'til the crave-smoulder flares, incendiary desire firing, fusing my lover and me. desire splays in the conception of its own demise. The Conception, the knowing unknowing life-play. playing out. to the nth, to the *Emm*th, degree.

89.

yes delay must end. must resist its continuance. must cease
and desist. it must end, to offer a new waiting hunger. but i have
delayed delay, renewed it with replay and resuscitation.
recitatif. made of delay an elaboration. an eternity. ostinato
delayed the inevitability of the closing down. why? i cannot
say. literally cannot say, not knowing, though i sow in the
field day after day. in delay we fence with death. fend off this
cocky mercenary. all life is delay. though the needle lays in
wait for us. yet we fence, and court immortality. make barriers
the length of a highway to protect ourselves and the animals.
soon though they will find a gap and cross the road. we will
pull onto the shoulder, show them to our son. antelope, elk
and mountain sheep. he will know them as trespassers.
interlopers in the human domain, though we'll try to explain.
he will breathe in their ear's range and they will consider him
dangerous despite his innocence, despite his lack of awareness of
delay. he will reach his hand toward their velvety noses in a
wish to belong to their world. to affirm his place in the world
of animals. this and his winter request for *body heat* are
young tentacles of desire reaching for contact, toward a time
when desire will propel him beyond himself. *if there is
eternity it is desire an air that enters all that is.* this is
poetry, but i would not claim that poetry is eternity. though it
could be. what should i say to my son? what will he say? i am
loping in a forest of ideas. i am a long way off. a long way
from understanding. i probe, i proffer, i submit offering. seek
opening. attempt to live in desire, in the absence of delay.

90.

    i am away. sunshine dazzles my room despite winter beyond my window and distance from my son. his light emanates into this small room where i write what detonates or trickles in my mind. his light shines from a school portrait where he sits at a wooden chair and table. he looks serious and intelligent, with a hint of smile. his living light shines in my mind where he dwells with vivacity. he is an emanance, an eminence, emancipating me from rigidities. i and my lover and the unknowable current made him, to toss ourselves beyond readiness, beyond predictability. into a beyond, there to make something new of ourselves. *in our culture of ready-mades, making anything is an accomplishment*. but what's accomplished is not ours. we can take no credit, but for allowing our desiring bodies to join on a candlelit night. he is a light beyond this, beyond any light i can bask in. he is shining into shades i'll not know. he is a light that, when i glimpse, dazzles my dimming sight, enlightens my room. en-lighten. em-lighten. *emeth* light. light of truth. emitting. enhancing me.

95. for Jill

i am invisible

     i reach into the space, the three-fold vortex. try to write the writing that comes before writing. words that pulse before thought. like the welling-up i had before i called it *love*. i would write from that buzz-place. wind at my window whining its chill deep into the bark of the tree shaking there. wind complaining through invisible cracks in the casement to shiver my neck.
                  it begins in the river. skin-bare in the summery waters, that joining of lovers.   everything is grey. winter resists departure, threatening. i am a prisoner. i am long away. i see you in photographs on my desk.   lover   son   each of you   alone.
                                        invisible
in this writing is what she meant   though in a room she is not inconspicuous. nothing is simple. all is a snaky river, or a labyrinth. labyrinthine, this existence. in the folding i intend no erasure. i've tightened my world to pretend i understand though here i admit i apprehend so little of the larger maze.   we came with force into each other's life, a force whose intent, though not known (to us) was to bring forth a son. i was stubborn. not given to union, or fidelity. she came with fire and torrent (to get my attention) and our feet swept from under us and we fell. gasped *love* as we spun, current-tossed.   first we lost one, the river-sown, summer one of watery names.   later we swam in a wintry bed at solstice to seed you. you, determined to be born.

the labyrinth has many surprises. a monster lives there. and we battle it to set you free. and our selves. i am still groping for the writing before the written. slipping on the slick of the known.   i'm scraping my old skin for each of you — lover, son. unveiling invisibilities. aiming for unprotection. seeking heat, a true and further keeling.

98.

    comes clear as I walk behind you tricycling. you, child, are spirit. in human form. with churning three-and-a-half year-old knees. wind bores a chill into my scarf-gaps. there is muck about. footing is unsure.
    comes clear. I am entrusted with care of the spirit living in your boy-shape. I scramble to meet you on purest ground. you are exuberance splashing your red and silver trike through lakes of snowmelt.
    comes clear that I expect a spirit to be serene. eight months ago you couldn't reach the pedals. two weeks ago you couldn't steer. you refused my help. the spirit wrestles with itself. in its skin. you grow. five days ago you turned and fell, bashing your shin.
    comes clear. this is the path of the spirit: to come pure into human form, to struggle in bodily confines bruised by the impurities of imperfect hosts. I am a flawed guardian. you struggle to live beyond the stain. today you pedal eleven blocks, speeding ahead of me.
    comes clear that I have stumbled into murky words. *spirit* and *purity*. I am naked and cluttered with assumption. I barely know what I mean, though I hear a distant whispering.
    comes clear. in my duty I meet your spirit's serenity, its fierceness, its purity. sky is streaking orange. sun will soon set. the body is an ageing spirit vessel, a husk soon shed. I must attend and see spirit-you pedalling like fury on your tricycle.

comes clear in the darkening. I call *it's time to turn around now, go home.* you complain, *no it's not dark. no!* you are a wilful child, resistant. I listen to know the complainant. I strain through impatience to meet the spirit in you, I am jarred, bent and straightened. lifted, I lean.

comes clear into incomprehension. no clarity but the effort toward.

notes on references and quoted lines

#14
heads are full of other people's words
Daphne Marlatt, *Ana Historic*, p.81. Coach House Press, Toronto, 1988.

#29
from the prisonhouse . . . world of speech.
Robert Kroetsch, *The Grammar of Silence*, p.93. Speaking of the character Niels in F. P. Grove's novel, *Settlers of the Marsh*. In *The Lovely Treachery of Words*, Oxford University Press, Toronto, 1989.

the cry of its occasion.
Gerald L. Bruns, *De Improvisatione*, in *Iowa Review 9*, Iowa, 1978.

#33
as your mother RK, does not remember . . . smiling, with her lips.
Robert Kroetsch, *Birthday, June 26 1983*, in *Advice to My Friends (Sounding the Name)*. Stoddart, Don Mills. 1985.

#45
everything we see could also be otherwise.
Ludwig Wittgenstein (tr. C.K Ogden), in *Tractatus Logico-Philosophicus*, Routledge & Kegan Paul Ltd., in association with Methuen Inc., New York. 1933.

#57
[saying] "ordinary" you draw . . . that is.
Found and then lost again, somewhere in the writings of bpNichol.

Generations Generated.
bpNichol, A performance text composed in 1977, unpublished, but notated in his 'Grey Notebook'. He performed this piece several times in the late 70s & 80s, and recorded it on his *Ear Rational* audiocassette (New Fire Tapes/Membrane Press).

#78
everyday talk cut off from true being
John Felstiner, *Paul Celan: Poet, Survivor, Jew*. p. 144-5. Yale University Press, New Haven/London. 1995.

#82
in the shape of seconds
Paul Celan, in *WHEN YOU LIE IN,* in *Atemwende*, p.255 in *Poems of Paul Celan*, Michael Hamburger, (tr.), Persea Books, New York. 1995.

#89
if there is eternity . . . ,
E.D. Blodgett, Jacques Brault, *Transfiguration,* p. 84, Editions du Noroit/Buschek Books, Saint-Hippolyte, QC. 1998.

#90
in our culture of ready-mades . . . accomplishment.
Daphne Marlatt, *Readings from the Labyrinth*, p.123. NeWest Press, Edmonton. 1998.

In the Acknowedgements
without a second thought, and *unpremeditated verse.*
Gerald L. Bruns, *De Improvisatione*, in *Iowa Review 9*, Iowa, 1978.

acknowledgements

Three extended conversations with Fred Wah in 1996 germinated seeds of ideas about poetic composition. These notions included: beginning "without a second thought," and improvisation leading to "unpremeditated verse." A bit later, in two walking chats, Daphne Marlatt emphasized the possibility of moving around in — not through — a compositional space. Fred, Daphne, I thank you for showing me openings to that place I'd been trying to conjure. I also wish to acknowledge Anne Szumigalski, John L. Clark, Susan Andrews Grace, and Hilary Clark for their invaluable comments and encouragement. The process was aided by financial assistance, from the Canada Council for the Arts and the Saskatchewan Arts Board, which enabled me to "purchase" time to write. And finally I must express my deep gratitude to J. Jill Robinson, my companion, enthusiast, and close reader, without whose participation this work would not exist. And then there is Emmett H Robinson Smith. . . .

Steven Ross Smith, Saskatoon, June 1999

*Some of these pieces previously appeared
in the following places:*

ice fog rises . . . , *the goldeneye* . . . , *open wide* . . . ,
published in *Contemporary Verse 2, Vol. 20, No.1.* Winnipeg.
1997.

9., 14., published in *Ledger Domain: An Anthology for Robert Kroetsch*, Trout Lily Press, Waterloo. 1997.

29., 33., published in *The New Quarterly, Vol. XVIII, No.1,* Waterloo.1998.

4., 8., 9., published in *Poetry Nation: The North American Anthology of Fusion Poetry*, Vehicule Press, Montreal. 1998.

41., published on the *East Village Poetry Web: Volume 4, The Poetries of Canada.* 1998.

Furrowed soil . . . , *soothing baby* . . . , *the heart radiant* . . . , *A white dusting* . . . , *ice fog rises* . . . , *the goldeneye* . . . , and *open wide* . . . , broadcast on CBC Radio 1 & 2, Saskatchewan, June 1999.